Where Are They?

Marcus Figorito

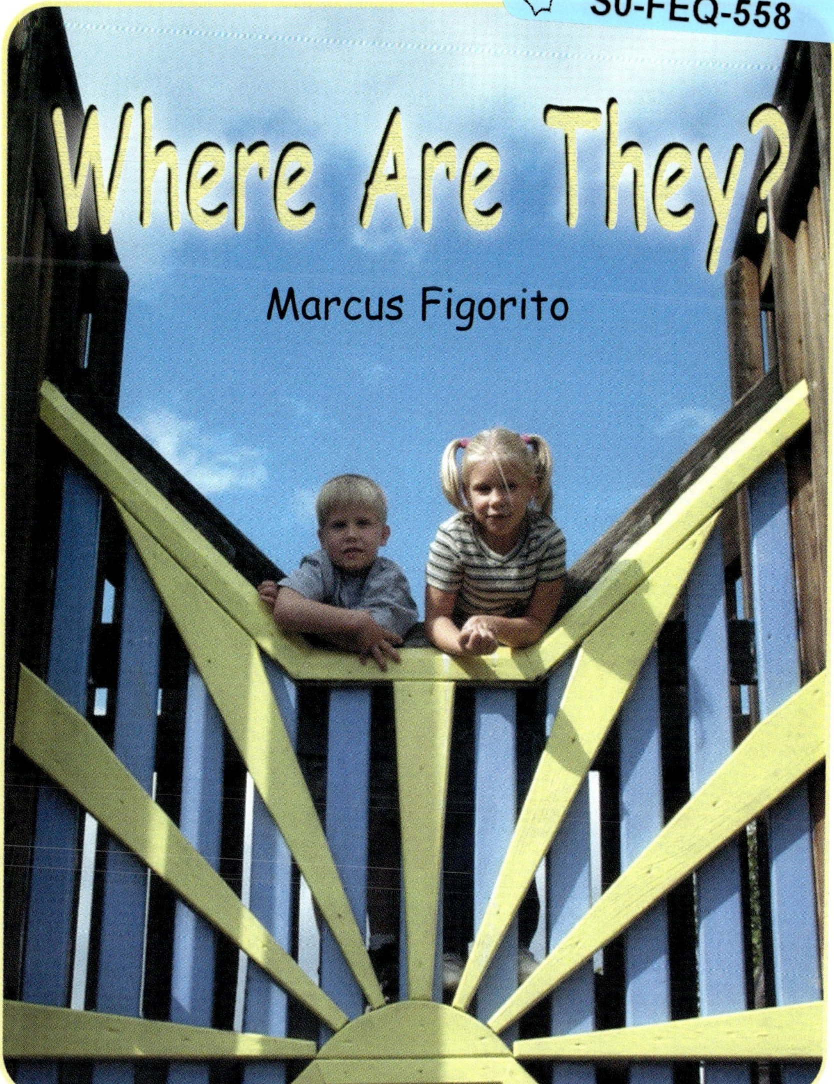

Rosen REAL READERS

Rosen Classroom Books & Materials
New York

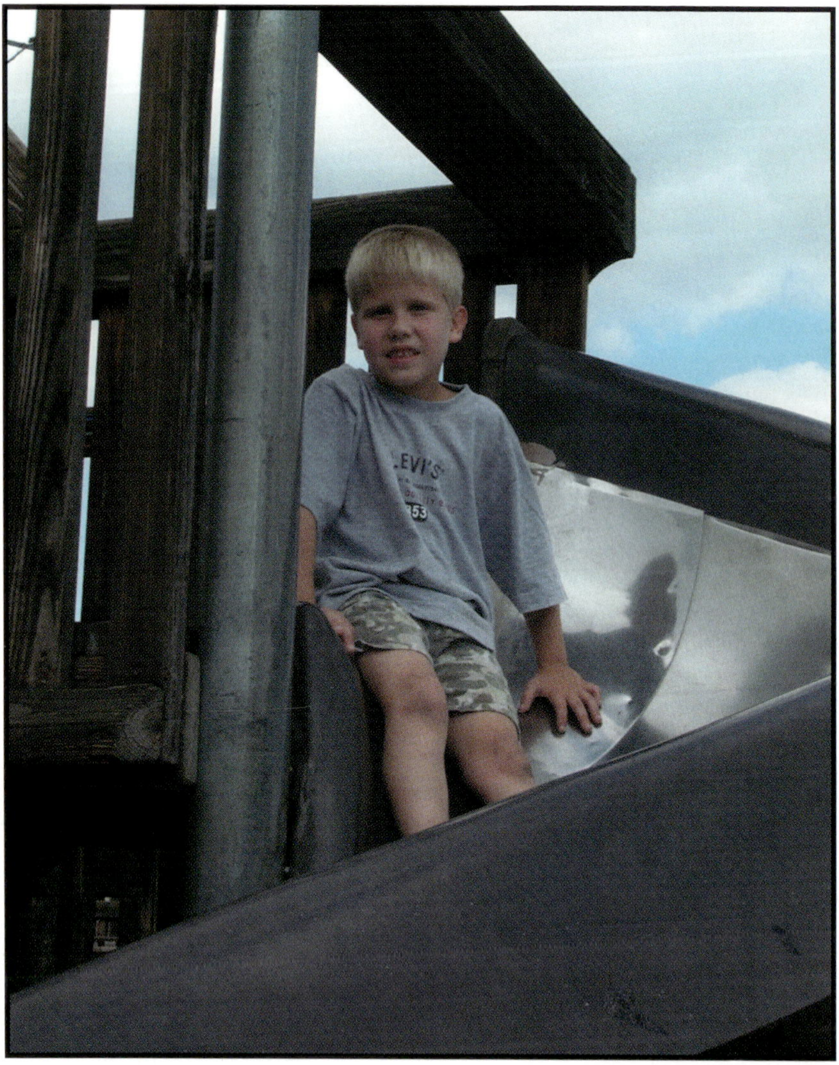

He is up.

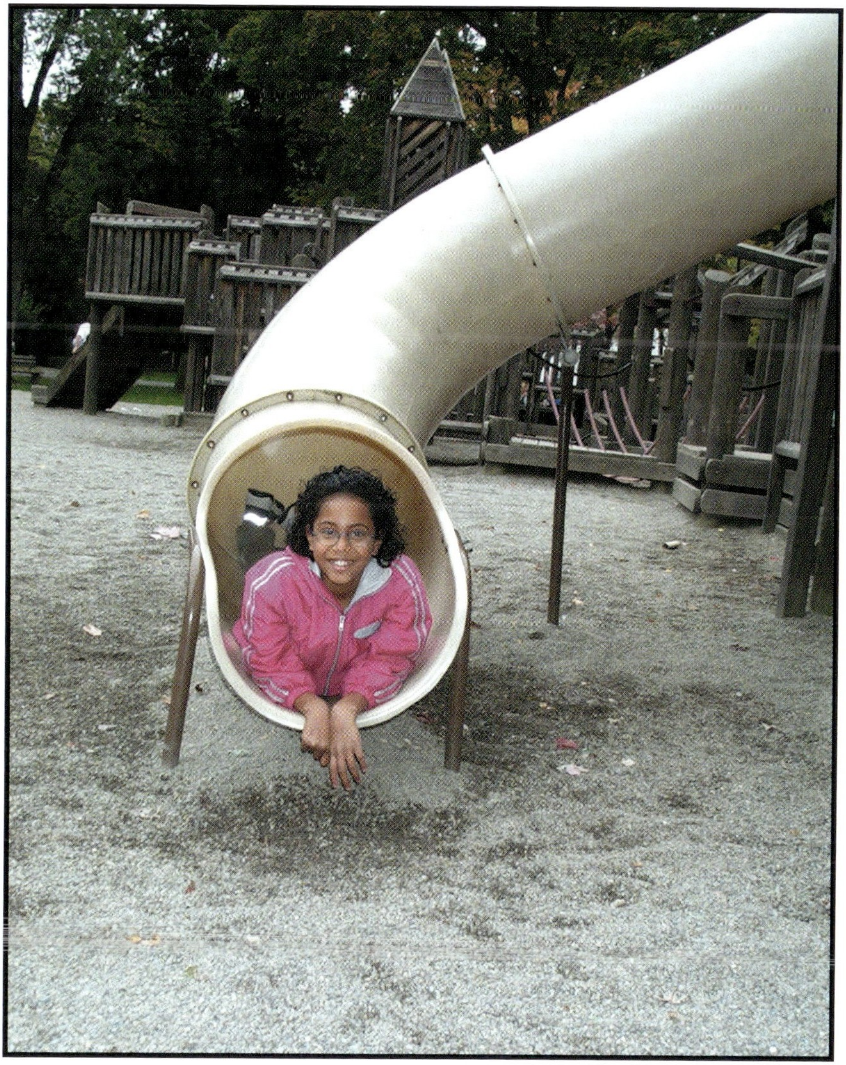

She is down.

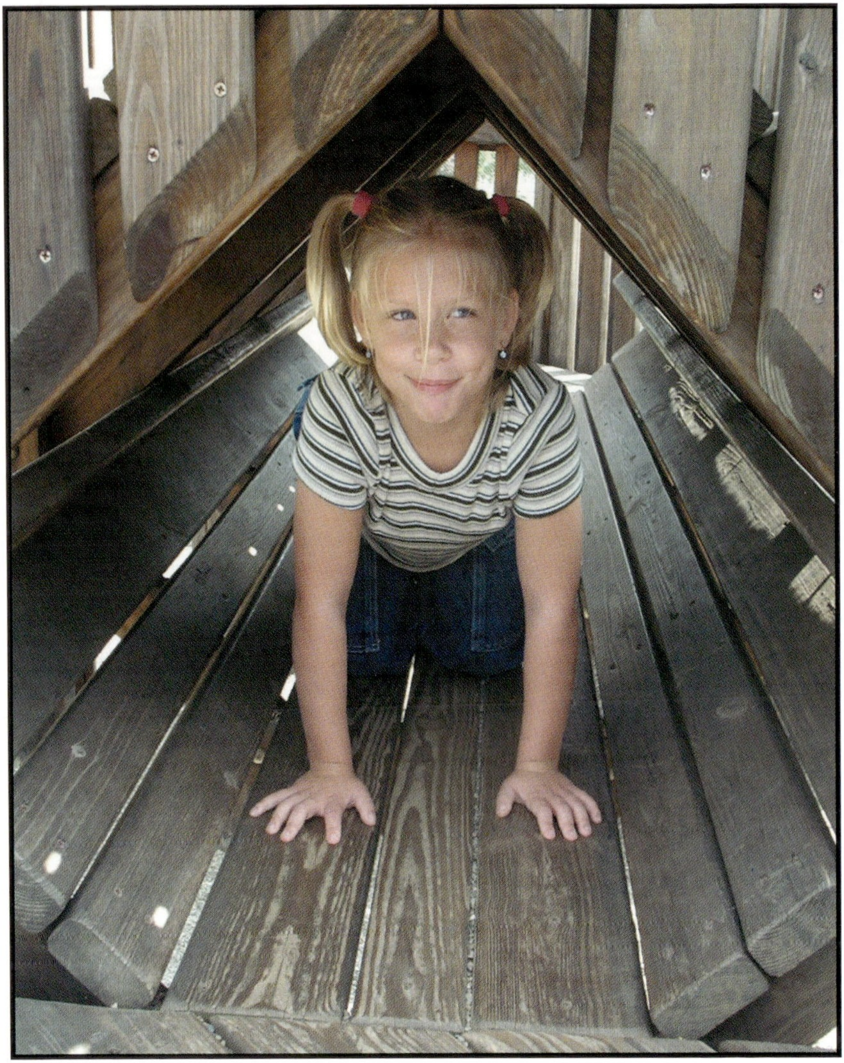

She is in.

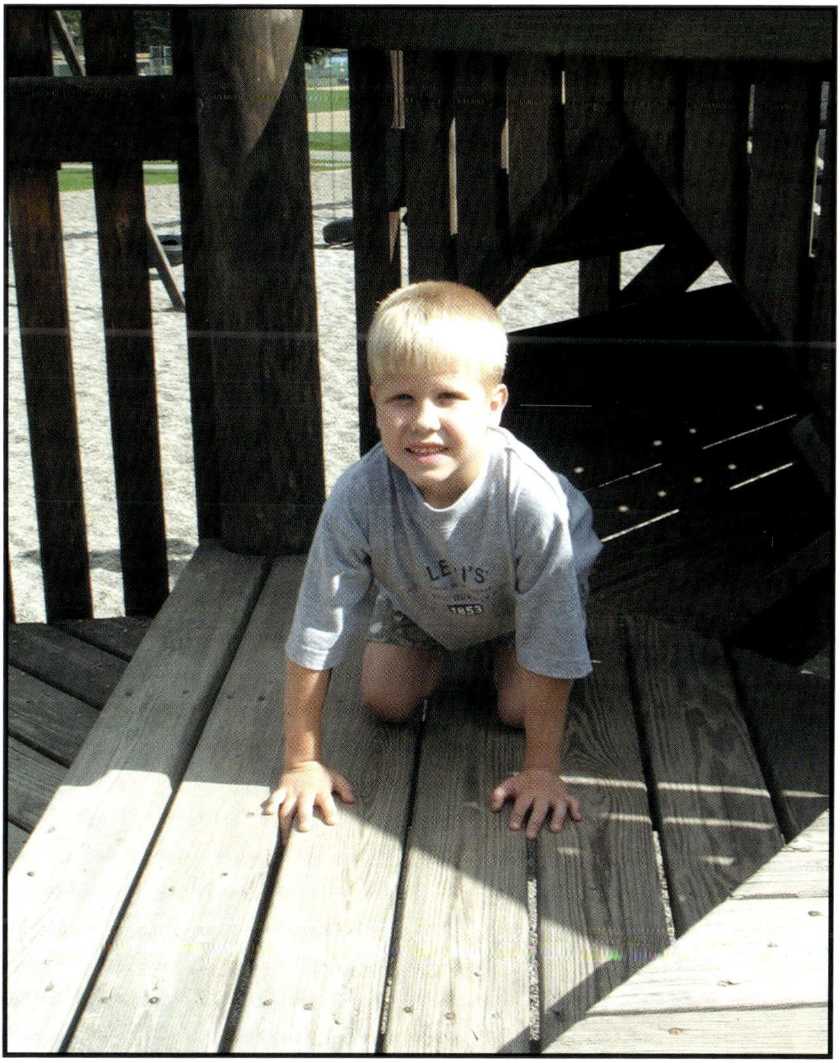

He is out.

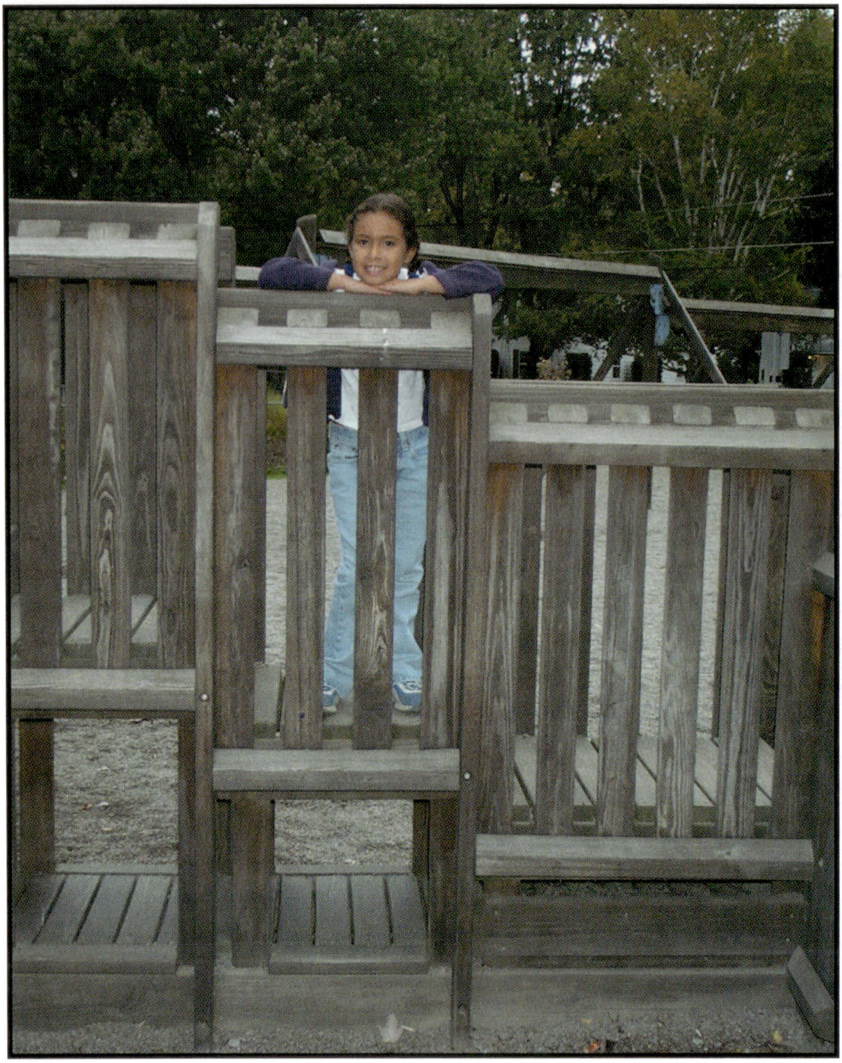

She is over.

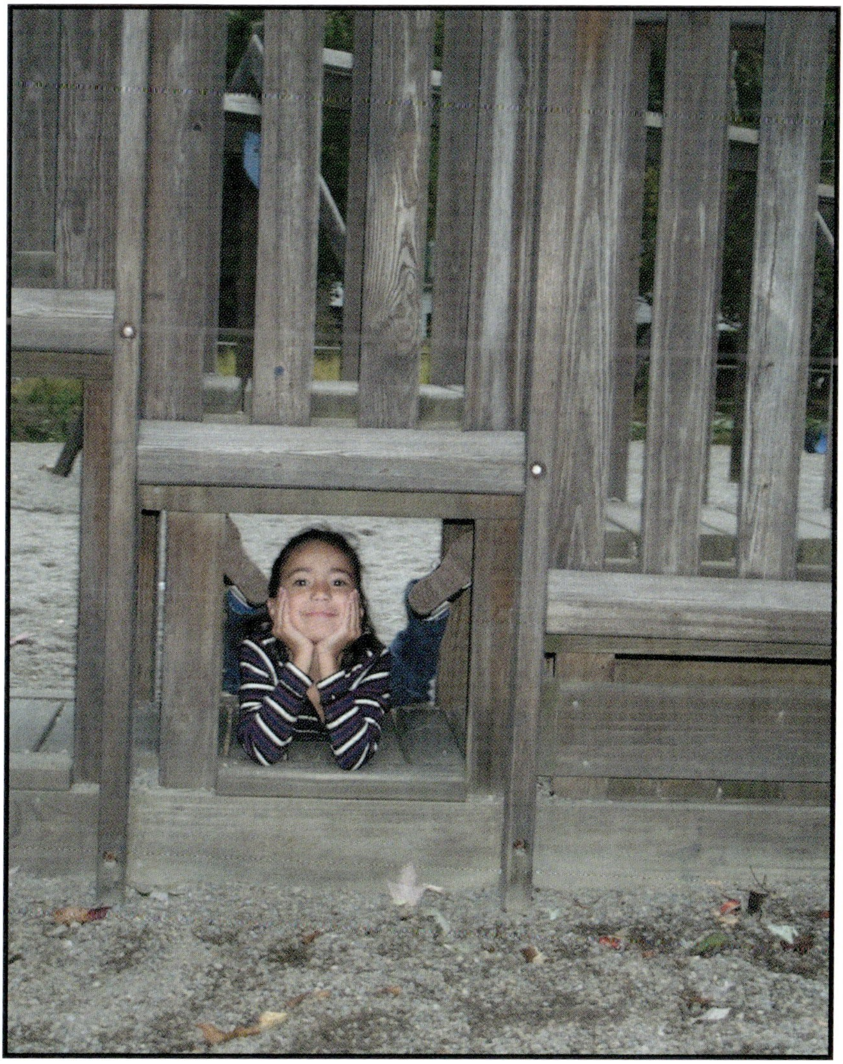

She is under.

Words to Know

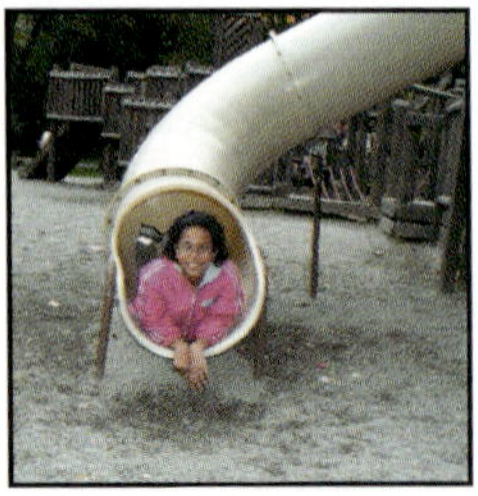

down

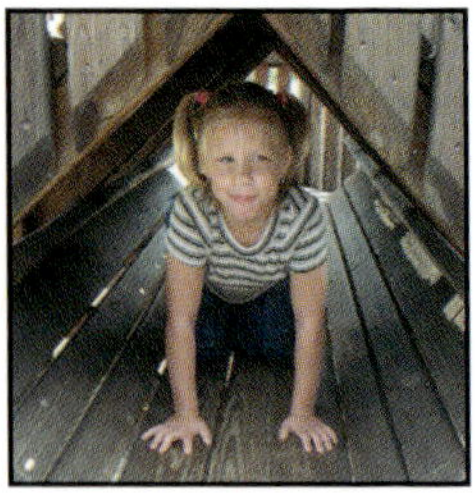

in

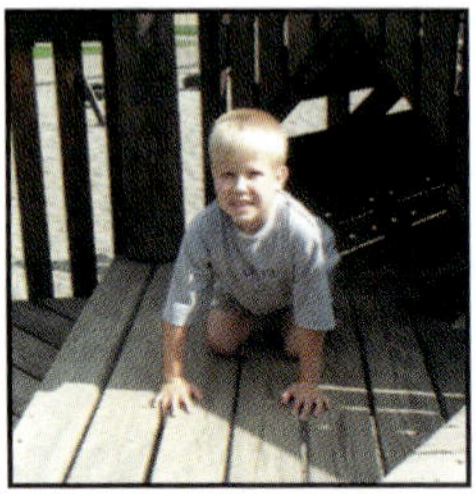

out

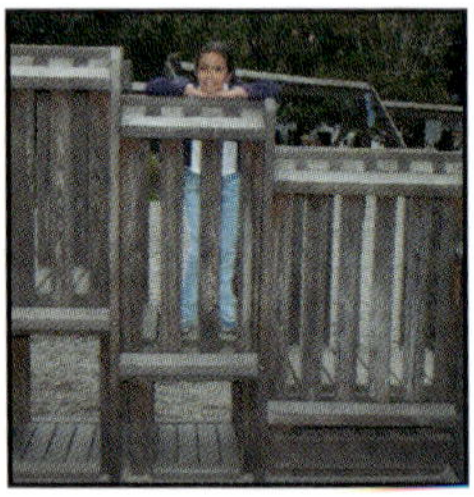

over

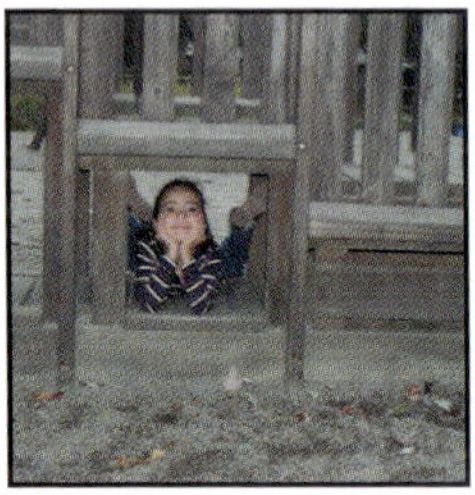

under

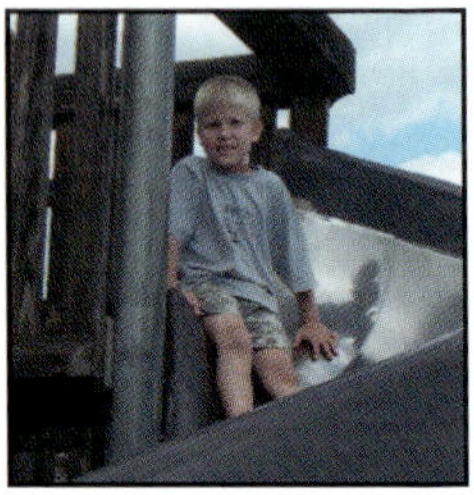

up